THE JOURNEY OF BRADLEY JOHN WALSH BIOGRAPHY

BY

ALBERT D. CHANEY

Copyright © 2024

All Rights Reserved.

No part of this book may be duplicated in any form, or by any electronic or mechanical means, including information storing and retrieval systems, without the author's written consent.

PREFACE

Individuals in the entertainment industry possess broad abilities and real charm that extend beyond the confines of their particular vocations. Bradley John Walsh is one such individual, a light whose rise through the ranks of television, acting, music, and beyond has left an everlasting stamp on the British entertainment scene.

This preface serves as the starting point for an exploration of Bradley John Walsh's life and career, a journey that delves into the depths of his early beginnings, navigates the highs and lows of his professional trajectory, and celebrates the enduring legacy he has carved for himself in the hearts of audiences all over the world.

As we begin on this journey, it is critical to recognize the significant influence Bradley John Walsh has had not only on the entertainment business, but also on the lives of many others who have been affected by his works. From modest beginnings to spectacular climb to popularity, Walsh's narrative is one of persistence, passion, and unflinching devotion to his profession.

Through the pages that follow, we take you on a captivating journey through Bradley John Walsh's life and career. From his early ambitions to his successes on stage and cinema, from laughter to tears, each chapter reveals a new dimension of his varied demeanor, providing insight into the man behind the limelight.

As we dive into Walsh's journey, we urge you to not only observe his achievements, but also to enjoy the essence of his spirit, which is laced with sincerity, kindness, and an unshakable devotion to delivering joy to audiences of all ages.

In commemorating Bradley John Walsh's life and legacy, we hope to not only pay tribute to a unique talent, but also to demonstrate the transforming power of entertainment, a force that crosses boundaries, unifies communities, and leaves an everlasting stamp on the fabric of society.

So, dear reader, as we turn the page and embark on this journey, let us celebrate the magic of storytelling, the brilliance of creativity, and pay tribute to Bradley John Walsh's incomparable legacy, which continues to shine brightly, illuminating the hearts and minds of all who have had the privilege of experiencing his artistry.

Welcome to the world of Bradley John Walsh, where dreams come true, laughter flows freely, and the spirit of entertainment has no boundaries.

Table of Contents

PREFACE 3
INTRODUCTION 11
CHAPTER ONE 17
   BRADLEY JOHN WALSH 17
CHAPTER TWO 22
   Early Life and Career Beginnings 22
CHAPTER THREE 28
   CHILDHOOD AND FAMILY
   BACKGROUND 28
      EDUCATIONAL AND EARLY
      INTERESTS 32
CHAPTER FOUR 37
   ENTRY TO SHOW BUSINESS 37
CHAPTER FIVE 42
   Rising Through the Rankings: Television
   Career 42
BREAKTHROUGH ROLES 48
CHAPTER SIX 56
   MUSIC CAREER AND DISCOGRAPHY . 56
      OTHER CREATIVE PURSUITS 60
CHAPTER SEVEN 65

BEHIND THE SCENES: PERSONAL LIFE
AND RELATIONSHIPS 65
PHILANTHROPIC ENDEAVOURS 71
CHALLENGES AND TRIUMPHS 76
CHAPTER EIGHT 82
IMPACT AND INFLUENCE 82
FANBASE AND PUBLIC PERCEPTIONS ... 87
AWARDS AND ACCOLADES 92
CONCLUSION 97
   Bradley John Walsh's Enduring Legacy 97

INTRODUCTION

Bradley John Walsh, a name synonymous with television, acting, music, and entertainment, is a figure whose multifarious abilities and charismatic personality have captivated audiences all over the world. From humble beginnings to household recognition, Walsh's path exemplifies the power of passion, perseverance, and pursuing one's ambitions.

In this introduction, we will go on a quest to discover the soul of Bradley John Walsh, the guy behind the numerous roles, captivating laughter, and limitless charm. We look at the fabric of his life, examining the formative experiences that influenced his path and the defining moments that brought him to fame.

Bradley John Walsh was born on June 4, 1960, in Watford, Hertfordshire. He grew up in a working-class household and learnt the principles of hard work, resilience, and tenacity from a young age. Despite early struggles and losses, Walsh had a profound passion for performing that drove him to pursue a career in entertainment.

As we progress through Walsh's life, we meet important situations that set him on the route to greatness. From his early efforts into show business, which included amateur dramatics and stand-up comedy, to his breakthrough performances on television, Walsh has demonstrated an unflinching dedication to his art and an instinctive ability to connect with viewers on a deep level.

Walsh rose to notoriety via his parts in renowned television dramas like "Coronation Street" and "Law & Order: UK," where his explosive performances demonstrated his flexibility as an actor and gained him critical acclaim. However, it was his work as the charming host of the game show "The Chase" that propelled Walsh to the heights of television fame, solidifying his legacy as one of Britain's most popular characters.

Walsh's abilities extend beyond his cinematic exploits, as he has achieved success as a singer and recording artist. With many albums under his belt and a knack for crooning timeless songs, Walsh has won over listeners with his beautiful voice and passionate performances.

Perhaps what distinguishes Bradley John Walsh is not his talent or awards, but the real warmth and genuineness with which he approaches everything he does. Walsh's contagious passion and down-to-earth charisma have won over admirers of all ages, whether he's entertaining millions on television, dazzles crowds on stage, or lends his voice to charity.

In the pages that follow, we welcome you to go on a voyage of discovery, one that honors Bradley John Walsh's life, legacy, and enduring spirit. From his modest origins to his stratospheric ascent to stardom, from the laughter he inspires to the joy he delivers, Walsh's narrative exemplifies the power of dreams, the enchantment of entertainment, and the human spirit's limitless potential.

So, dear reader, join us as we uncover the mystery of Bradley John Walsh, a man whose abilities are limitless, whose heart has no limitations, and his legacy shines brilliantly as a light of inspiration for future generations. Welcome to the world of Bradley John Walsh, where dreams may fly, laughter reigns supreme, and the spirit of entertainment has no boundaries.

CHAPTER ONE

BRADLEY JOHN WALSH

Bradley John Walsh is a talented British artist recognized for his work in television, acting, singing, and hosting. Walsh was born on June 4, 1960, in Watford, Hertfordshire, and has had a long career spanning several decades, winning accolades for his explosive performances and magnetic character.

Growing up in a working-class household, Bradley John Walsh learnt the importance of hard work and tenacity from a young age. Walsh's early years were distinguished by a penchant for performing, as he actively participated in amateur dramatics and honed his abilities as a comedian. Despite encountering hurdles such as dyslexia, Walsh remained determined to pursue a career in entertainment.

Walsh's television career began with roles in comic series and dramas, demonstrating his flexibility as an actor. He rose to prominence for his parts in famous television shows such as "Coronation Street" and "Law & Order: UK," where his captivating performances garnered him critical praise.

However, Walsh's career as host of the game program "The Chase" propelled him to global prominence. Since joining the show in 2009, Walsh has been identified with it, attracting fans with his quick wit, friendly manner, and engaging hosting style.

Bradley John Walsh had a successful acting career that includes film, television, and stage roles, in addition to his television work. He has demonstrated his emotional versatility in films such as "Torn," "Sun Trap," and "Doctor Who," receiving plaudits for his captivating performances.

In addition to acting and presenting, Walsh has attempted a music career. He has published multiple CDs of renditions of great songs, demonstrating his deep voice and musical ability. Walsh's musical career has further endeared him to viewers by showcasing his flexibility as an entertainer.

Bradley John Walsh is well-known for his humanitarian activities and engagement in charity organizations. He has given his support to a variety of groups, utilizing his position to promote awareness and cash for critical social concerns.

In his personal life, Walsh is noted for his down-to-earth approach and genuine kindness, which attract him to both fans and colleagues. He is a dedicated family guy who balances his profession with his responsibilities to his loved ones.

Legacy and Influence: Bradley John Walsh's influence in the entertainment world is unmistakable. Walsh's riveting performances on screen, as well as his engaging personality as a television host and musician, have made an unforgettable impression on audiences throughout the world. His long legacy reflects his brilliance, commitment, and undying enthusiasm for his profession.

CHAPTER TWO

Early Life and Career Beginnings

Bradley John Walsh was born June 4, 1960, in Watford, Hertfordshire, England. Walsh grew up in a working-class home with little resources and a close-knit community. He had a natural talent for performing and entertaining at a young age, and he aspired to work in the arts.

Despite overcoming hurdles such as dyslexia, Walsh stayed determined to achieve in the entertainment industry. During his early years, he actively engaged in local amateur dramatics and refined his humorous abilities by doing stand-up comedy at numerous locations. These early experiences not only allowed Walsh to develop his abilities, but also established in him a strong work ethic and perseverance that would determine his future professional path.

Walsh's professional entertainment career began in the 1980s, when he made his television debut on the British soap opera "Coronation Street." Although his early positions were tiny, they gave vital experience and opened the path for future chances in the sector. Walsh's innate charm and humorous timing quickly drew the attention of casting directors, resulting in roles in prominent television sitcoms and dramas.

Throughout the 1990s and early 2000s, Walsh expanded his acting resume with appearances in a variety of television shows, demonstrating his flexibility as a performer. During this time, he made cameos on series including "Lock, Stock...," "The Bill," and "The Sarah Jane Adventures." Walsh's ability to fluidly switch between humorous and tragic parts cemented his reputation as a skilled actor capable of portraying varied characters with depth and sensitivity.

In addition to his television work, Walsh dabbled in theater acting, performing in plays around the United Kingdom. His theater credits include parts in plays like "One Flew Over the Cuckoo's Nest" and "The Ragged Trousered Philanthropists," where he was praised for his captivating performances and stage presence.

Despite his success as an actor, Walsh's path in the entertainment world was not without hurdles. Like many aspiring artists, he experienced times of uncertainty and rejection while navigating the unpredictable nature of show business with tenacity and persistence. Walsh's undying enthusiasm for his profession, along with his unflinching devotion to improving his abilities, eventually moved him ahead, resulting to breakthrough chances that would rocket him to greater fame in the years to come.

Bradley John Walsh's career progressed, and he quickly embarked on new enterprises that cemented his standing as a beloved personality in the entertainment industry. Walsh's early life and professional beginnings lay the groundwork for a productive and long-lasting path distinguished by skill, determination, and a real passion for the art of performance.

CHAPTER THREE

CHILDHOOD AND FAMILY BACKGROUND

Bradley John Walsh's childhood in Watford, Hertfordshire, England, was influenced by the ideals established by his close-knit family and the realities of a working-class household. Walsh was born on June 4, 1960, into a caring family setting that encouraged his early interests and developed his developing skills.

Growing up, Walsh had a strong link with his parents and siblings, cherishing the basic joys of family life despite the obstacles of little resources. His youth was marked by a strong feeling of community and togetherness, with family gatherings and shared meals serving as the foundation of their tight familial relationships.

As the eldest of numerous siblings, Walsh accepted a position of responsibility within the family, demonstrating a natural proclivity for leadership and fostering his innate sense of empathy and compassion. His early years were blessed by his parents' love and guidance, whose encouragement and support played a critical part in defining his dreams and goals.

Despite the limits of a working-class background, Walsh's parents instilled in him the virtues of hard work, integrity, and tenacity, emphasizing the significance of following one's passions with devotion and drive. Their unshakable conviction in Walsh's potential inspired him, igniting his aspirations of a career in the arts and giving him the confidence to follow his goals despite all odds.

Throughout his boyhood, Walsh shown a natural talent for performance and entertainment, attracting family and friends with his humorous antics and instinctive charisma. Walsh's early creative expressions, whether amusing visitors with impromptu skits or demonstrating his knack for imitation, foreshadowed a successful career.

As Walsh traversed the complications of adolescence, he found consolation and meaning in his artistic activities, looking to the realm of entertainment for self-expression and pleasure. His enthusiasm for performing became stronger with age, propelling him to seek possibilities for artistic expression and begin on a journey that would eventually bring him to the pinnacle of achievement in the entertainment industry.

In reflecting on his childhood and family history, Bradley John Walsh recognizes how his upbringing shaped his ideals, objectives, and worldview. His early years established in him a strong awareness for the value of family, the strength of perseverance, and the transformational potential of pursuing one's passions with steadfast commitment.

EDUCATIONAL AND EARLY INTERESTS

Bradley John Walsh's transformation from a young, ambitious performer to a multidimensional entertainer was formed by a combination of formal schooling and early interests that fueled his enthusiasm for the arts.

Walsh's early schooling at Watford, Hertfordshire, provided a solid basis for his future undertakings. Despite dyslexia-related obstacles, Walsh displayed a sharp intellect and a voracious thirst for learning, excelling in areas that grabbed his interest and cultivating his artistic talents through extracurricular activities.

Although Walsh's official education equipped him with essential skills and information, it was his experiences outside of the classroom that truly piqued his interest in the arts and laid the groundwork for his future career in entertainment.

Bradley John Walsh has always had a passion for performing and entertainment, expressing his originality and captivating audiences with his charm.

One of Walsh's first passions was comedy, and he acquired a talent for making others laugh with his wit, humor, and comedic timing. Walsh's early explorations into comedy, whether amusing friends and family with impromptu skits or developing his abilities as a rising comic at local comedy clubs, gave him a platform to exhibit his talent and create his distinct humorous style.

In addition to comedy, Walsh acquired a love of music, finding consolation and inspiration in the power of song and melody. From singing along to his favorite recordings to exploring different musical genres and styles, Walsh's love of music became an integral part of his personality and a form of creative expression that would eventually materialize in his career as a recording artist.

Furthermore, Walsh's love with the realm of theater and performing arts spurred his ambition to investigate the possibilities of storytelling and character representation. Walsh's early theatrical experiences, whether he was immersed in dramatic parts or experimenting with improvisational theater, provided him with a platform to improve his acting talents and acquire a profound passion for the profession.

CHAPTER FOUR

ENTRY TO SHOW BUSINESS

Bradley John Walsh's entry into the entertainment industry was distinguished by a mix of skill, tenacity, and a sequence of formative events that drove him from a young, aspiring performer to a diversified entertainer with a thriving career in television, acting, music, and hosting.

Bradley John Walsh has a natural talent for performing and entertainment at an early age. He found delight in expressing his inventiveness and captivating audiences with his charisma. His early interests in humor, music, and theater served as a basis for his future career in the entertainment industry.

Walsh began his career in stand-up comedy, honing his abilities in local clubs and events. He also dabbled with amateur drama. His sharp wit, humor, and engaging stage presence rapidly drew notice, cementing his status as a bright new artist on the comedy circuit.

In addition to stand-up comedy, Walsh dabbled in amateur dramatics, immersing himself in the realm of theater and performance art. Walsh's amateur dramatics experiences, whether in school plays or local theater productions, presented him with great opportunity to hone his acting abilities and pursue his passion for storytelling.

Bradley's television debut and early roles. John Walsh made his television debut in the 1980s, with a role in the long-running British soap opera "Coronation Street." Although his early appearances were brief, they acted as a springboard for Walsh to demonstrate his skill and acquire attention in the entertainment world.

Throughout the 1990s and early 2000s, Walsh expanded his acting resume with appearances in a variety of television shows, demonstrating his flexibility as a performer. During this time, he appeared on sitcoms including "Lock, Stock...," "The Bill," and "The Sarah Jane Adventures," where he stood out for his riveting performances and dynamic range as an actor.

Breakthrough Opportunities: Despite hurdles and disappointments, Bradley John Walsh remained determined to excel in show business. His breakthrough performances allowed him to exhibit his comic talent and magnetic personality, resulting in significant recognition and admiration from audiences and industry peers alike.

Walsh's greatest significant success came as the presenter of the popular game show "The Chase," which he joined in 2009. His quick wit, amiable manner, and engaging presenting style helped him become a household name, propelling him to worldwide popularity and cementing his place as one of Britain's most cherished television personalities.

CHAPTER FIVE

Rising Through the Rankings: Television Career

Bradley John Walsh's television career showcases his flexibility, charm, and unquestionable aptitude as an entertainer. From his early appearances in British soap operas to his legendary role as a television presenter, Walsh's rise through the ranks of television has been defined by a string of remarkable performances and unforgettable moments that have won him over viewers all over the globe.

In the 1980s, Welsh's television career took off with a recurrent part on the popular British serial opera "Coronation Street." His depiction of Danny Baldwin, a charming and often controversial figure, demonstrated Walsh's acting abilities and established the framework for his future success in the profession. His role on "Coronation Street" won him critical praise and vital exposure in the television industry.

Throughout the 1990s and early 2000s, Bradley John Walsh appeared in a variety of television shows across different genres. He demonstrated his flexibility as an actor by appearing in dramas, comedies, and crime dramas, receiving recognition for his ability to provide depth and subtlety to a diverse spectrum of characters.

Walsh's major television credits during this era include appearances in shows such as "Lock, Stock...," a criminal drama series based on the successful film, in which he played Jack Quinn. He also appeared in "The Bill," a long-running police procedural series, and "The Sarah

Jane Adventures," a science fiction show geared for younger viewers.

Bradley hosts and presents ventures. John Walsh's most notable contributions to the television profession came from his work as a host and presenter. Walsh became the presenter of the famous game show "The Chase" in 2009, cementing his reputation as a popular television personality. His quick wit, amiable manner, and contagious energy attracted him to fans, making him a key component of the series' success.

As host of "The Chase," Walsh was recognized for his engaging interaction with competitors, humorous banter with the show's regular quizmasters, and genuine excitement for the game. His magnetic personality and natural charm helped to boost the show's appeal, garnering him awards and distinction as one of Britain's most adored television hosts.

In addition to his job on "The Chase," Walsh has hosted a number of television series, award ceremonies, and reality challenges. His flexibility as a presenter has cemented his image as an entertainer who can flourish in a variety of television platforms.

Legacy in Television: Bradley John Walsh's television career demonstrates his ongoing influence on the business. Walsh's contributions to television, from debut parts in soap operas to memorable hosting stints, have made an unforgettable impression on viewers throughout the world. His versatility as an actor, allied with his magnetic presence as a presenter, has solidified his place as one of Britain's most adored television characters, assuring his legacy in television history.

BREAKTHROUGH ROLES

Bradley John Walsh's rise in the entertainment business was fueled by a string of breakthrough roles that displayed his ability, flexibility, and captivating screen presence. From his early success in soap operas to his famous image as a television presenter, Walsh's rise through the ranks of show business is marked by watershed moments that cemented his place as a household figure.

1. "Coronation Street" (2004-2006): Walsh's breakout role was as Danny Baldwin in the British serial series "Coronation Street." When Walsh joined the cast in 2004, his character rapidly became a fan favorite, enthralling viewers with his engaging presence and fascinating tale. Danny Baldwin, the leader of the Baldwin family and proprietor of the Underworld plant, was a complicated character whose moral ambiguity and emotional arcs exemplified Walsh's acting versatility. His exceptional performance on "Coronation Street" gained him critical praise and global

exposure, establishing the groundwork for Walsh's future success in the profession.

2. "The Chase" (2009 Present):

Another critical time in Bradley. John Walsh's career began with his stint as presenter of the successful game show "The Chase." Walsh joined the program in 2009, and his contagious energy, quick wit, and pleasant personality won over fans, making him an important element of the show's success. As host of "The Chase," Walsh was recognized for his engaging connection with competitors, amusing exchanges with the show's regular quizmasters, and genuine excitement for the game. His magnetic personality and natural charm helped to boost the show's appeal, garnering him awards and distinction as one of Britain's most adored television hosts. "The Chase" is now one of the most popular quiz shows on British television, and Walsh's role as host remains a defining element of his career.

3. Bradley John Walsh starred as Graham O'Brien in the science fiction series "Doctor Who" from 2018 to 2019. Walsh, who joined the ensemble in 2018 alongside Jodie Whittaker's Thirteenth Doctor, was

acclaimed for her depiction of Graham's warmth, comedy, and emotional depth. Graham, a former bus driver and Ryan Sinclair's step-grandfather, provided a genuine humanity to the show's ensemble, which resonated with viewers and earned Walsh considerable praise for his portrayal. His time on "Doctor Who" demonstrated Walsh's flexibility as an actor and cemented his place as a notable figure in the world of British television.

4. Law & Order: UK (2009-2014): Walsh played a key role in the British adaption of the popular American

criminal drama series "Law & Order: UK." He played Detective Sergeant Ronnie Brooks, an experienced detective with a keen intellect and a sympathetic heart. Walsh's depiction of Ronnie Brooks was praised for its complexity and depth, cementing his reputation as a superb actor capable of commanding the screen in serious parts. Walsh's appearance on "Law & Order: UK" increased his television resume and demonstrated his flexibility as a crime procedural actor.

5. Guest Appearances and Panel Shows: Bradley John Walsh has made several guest appearances on TV

programs and panel shows, demonstrating his comic aptitude and improvisational abilities. Walsh has proved his flexibility as an artist by appearing on talk programs and engaging in comic panel shows. His guest performances have frequently been distinguished by his quick wit, contagious humor, and magnetic personality, winning him admiration from both audiences and other comedians.

6. Musical Performances and Variety Shows: In addition to hosting and presenting, Bradley John Walsh has performed music on many TV shows.

He has performed musical pieces on shows such as "The Royal Variety Performance," which is an annual variety event showcasing top performers. Walsh's musical performances demonstrate his versatility as an artist and ability to captivate listeners with his soulful voice and charming stage presence.

CHAPTER SIX

MUSIC CAREER AND DISCOGRAPHY

Bradley John Walsh's music career demonstrates his numerous abilities as an artist, including his soulful voice and musical diversity. Walsh's music career has been defined by a passion for music and a true love of singing, from the release of CDs comprising renditions of great songs to live performances on stage.

1. Albums: Bradley John Walsh's debut album "Chasing Dreams" was published in 2016. The album contains covers of famous songs from the Great American Songbook, such as "That's Life," "Mr. Bojangles," and "Luck Be a Lady." Walsh's soulful voice and passionate interpretations breathe new life into these old songs, achieving both critical praise and commercial success.

"When You're Smiling" (2017): Following the popularity of his first album, Walsh published his second album, "When You're Smiling," in 2017. The album follows in the footsteps of its predecessor, with Walsh's versions of great standards including "When You're Smiling," "Can't Help Falling in Love," and "Beyond the Sea." Walsh captivates listeners with his soft voice and passionate delivery, while also paying respect to great melodies that have stood the test of time.

"Anticipation" (2020): Bradley John Walsh's third album, "Anticipation," is a compilation of iconic songs from the 1970s and 1980s. Walsh's broad musical interests are showcased on the album, which includes tunes ranging from pop and rock to soul and Motown. Songs such as "This Is My Life," "Tyrin' to Get the Feeling Again," and "Lovely Day" showcase Walsh's broad vocal range and ability to infuse each performance with passion and emotion.

2. Live Performances: Beyond studio records, Bradley John Walsh has demonstrated his musical abilities through live performances on stage. He has performed at a variety of musical venues and music festivals, attracting listeners with his beautiful voice, engaging stage presence, and genuine commitment to the music.

Walsh's live performances demonstrate his flexibility as a musician as well as his genuine enjoyment of performing music in front of live audiences.

3. Television Appearances: Bradley John Walsh has performed on shows including "The Royal Variety Performance" and "Tonight at the London Palladium." His participation on these shows have helped him to reach a larger audience and share his love of music with people around the country.

OTHER CREATIVE PURSUITS

Beyond his successful careers in acting, presenting, and singing, Bradley John Walsh has pursued a variety of other creative projects, showcasing his flexibility and enthusiasm for the arts. Walsh's broad creative pursuits, which include writing and producing, demonstrate his versatile talent and entrepreneurial energy.

1. Writing: Bradley. John Walsh has taken up writing, demonstrating his ingenuity and narrative ability. He has written various books, including autobiography, fiction, and children's literature. Walsh's work includes personal tales, observations, and

musings on his life and career, giving readers a view into his experiences and opinions.

2. Producing: Walsh uses his professional knowledge and artistic vision to deliver intriguing tales on screen. As a producer, he works with writers, directors, and other creatives to create projects that span several genres and platforms. Walsh's producing efforts demonstrate his entrepreneurial zeal and dedication to promoting various perspectives in the entertainment business.

3. Philanthropy and Charity Work: In addition to his artistic interests, Bradley John Walsh actively supports many causes and organizations through his platform. He takes part in fundraising events, philanthropic projects, and advocacy campaigns, using his influence to make a good difference in society and contribute to important causes.

4. Entrepreneurship: In addition to working in the entertainment sector, Walsh has explored and invested in business initiatives that match with his interests and principles. Walsh's entrepreneurial initiatives, which include creating his own production

firm, investigating prospects in the hotel sector, and investing in creative companies, highlight his commercial acumen and forward-thinking approach.

5. Public Speaking and Mentoring: Bradley John Walsh shares his knowledge and skills with emerging artists, entrepreneurs, and industry professionals. Through workshops, seminars, and speaking engagements, he motivates and enables people to follow their interests, overcome obstacles, and accomplish their creative and entertainment ambitions.

CHAPTER SEVEN

BEHIND THE SCENES: PERSONAL LIFE AND RELATIONSHIPS

Bradley John Walsh's personal life combines career accomplishment, family values, and a strong interest in philanthropy. Despite his hectic schedule in the entertainment world, Walsh lives a balanced life, valuing his ties with loved ones and actively participating in humanitarian causes.

1. Family Life: Bradley John Walsh's personal life revolves around his close family. He prioritizes his ties with his wife, Donna Derby, and his children, and cherishes the time they spend together despite his demanding profession. Walsh frequently speaks affectionately about his family in interviews, emphasizing the significance of their love and support in his life.

2. Philanthropy and Charity Work: Walsh utilizes his position to assist issues he cares about. He takes part in fundraising events, charity auctions, and advocacy campaigns, using his influence to generate awareness and support for organizations that promote healthcare, children's welfare, and education.

3. Hobbies and Interests: Beside his professional work, Bradley John Walsh pursues hobbies and interests to enhance his life and give leisure. He is a passionate sports fan, having a particular fondness for football and golf. Walsh also likes spending time

outside, whether hiking, gardening, or visiting new places with his family.

4. Maintaining Work-Life Balance: Despite his busy schedule in the entertainment sector, Walsh values a good work-life balance. He appreciates spending time with his family and makes an effort to be present for significant milestones and events in their life. Walsh's ability to balance his business and personal lives demonstrates his devotion to developing meaningful relationships and finding fulfillment outside of his job.

Bradley John Walsh, although being a well-known personality in the entertainment business, prioritizes his personal privacy. He likes to keep information about his family and personal connections private, instead focusing on his professional and charity pursuits. Despite the public spotlight, Walsh remains grounded and emphasizes solitude and limits in his personal life.

6. Legacy and ideals: Bradley John Walsh's personal and professional career reflects his ideals of family, generosity, and humility. He aims to have a good influence on the world

via both his entertainment profession and his charity initiatives. Walsh's legacy goes beyond his accomplishments in the entertainment business, including his dedication to making a difference in the lives of others and cherishing the connections that are most important to him.

PHILANTHROPIC ENDEAVOURS

Bradley John Walsh's charitable initiatives demonstrate his commitment to making a good difference in the world and helping those in need. Throughout his career, Walsh has actively participated in a variety of philanthropic activities and organizations, using his platform to promote awareness and support for issues near to his heart.

1. Healthcare Charities: Walsh is a strong supporter of healthcare charities, emphasizing the need of ensuring access to decent treatment for those in need. He has taken part in fundraising events and charity auctions to support hospitals, medical research, and projects to improve healthcare services for both children and adults.

2. Children's Welfare: Bradley John Walsh, a parent and family guy, is passionate about children's welfare. He has supported groups that help vulnerable children, such as those battling poverty, disease, and abuse.

Walsh's efforts have included fundraising drives, awareness-raising projects, and trips to children's hospitals and orphanages to console and support young patients and their families.

3. Education projects: Walsh believes in the transforming power of education and has sponsored projects that provide opportunity for children and young people from underprivileged situations. He has contributed to scholarship programs, school building projects, and literacy initiatives, emphasizing the value of education in breaking the cycle of

poverty and encouraging future generations to attain their full potential.

4. Animal Welfare: Walsh is an advocate for animal welfare and has worked to increase awareness about the need to protect wildlife and domestic animals. He has funded animal rescue organizations, wildlife conservation projects, and programs to promote ethical pet ownership. Walsh's enthusiasm for animals is obvious in his advocacy work, which aims to make the world a better place for all species, large and little.

5. Bradley John Walsh advocates for resolving homelessness and poverty by providing compassionate assistance and services to people and families experiencing economic distress. He has sponsored efforts that provide shelter, food, job training, and other critical services to people battling homelessness and poverty. Walsh's activism strives to raise awareness about the structural challenges that contribute to homelessness and poverty, as well as to rally support for comprehensive solutions that address the underlying causes.

6. Bradley John Walsh supports charitable causes and has attended fundraising events and performances to raise cash and awareness for many organizations. He has played at charity concerts, organized fundraising galas, and taken part in televised charity events, using his ability and platform to positively touch the lives of others.

CHALLENGES AND TRIUMPHS

Bradley John Walsh's career in the entertainment industry has been filled with achievements as well as setbacks that have challenged his endurance and tenacity. From managing the industry's competitive nature to overcoming personal hurdles, Walsh's career has demonstrated his resilience and ability to overcome hardship.

Challenge 1: Early Career Struggles. Bradley John Walsh, like many aspiring actors, encountered early-career hurdles such as gaining auditions, landing jobs, and establishing himself in a tough business. He faced rejection and failures along the road, which challenged his drive and perseverance to follow his passion for acting.

2. Typecasting: As an actor, Walsh experienced the issue of being typecast in specific parts, especially at the beginning of his career. Breaking free from prejudices and broadening his horizons as a performer took effort and a desire to take on varied parts that demonstrated his flexibility.

3. Balancing Work and Personal Life: With a rigorous schedule in the entertainment business, Bradley John Walsh had to strike a balance between his professional and personal life. Maintaining a healthy work-life balance necessitated rigorous prioritizing and time management to

allow him to spend adequate time to his family and personal interests.

4. Public criticism: As a public person, Walsh has had to navigate public criticism and media attention. Maintaining privacy and boundaries in the face of intense public scrutiny can be difficult, necessitating perseverance and a strong sense of self to endure the demands of fame and popularity.

Triumphs:

1. Breakout Role: Bradley John Walsh's career has been highlighted

by many breakout performances that have demonstrated his ability and range as an actor. From his depiction of Danny Baldwin in "Coronation Street" to his role as Detective Sergeant Ronnie Brooks in "Law & Order: UK," Walsh's performances have gained him critical praise and cemented his reputation as a skilled actor.

2. Hosting Success: Walsh's hosting job on "The Chase" has been a career highlight, bringing him global exposure and admiration as a television personality. His entertaining presenting manner and interaction with competitors have

boosted the show's appeal and made him a beloved character on British television.

3. Musical Career: Bradley John Walsh's music career has been another achievement, with his CDs "Chasing Dreams," "When You're Smiling," and "Anticipation" demonstrating his musical skill and reaching a large audience. His beautiful voice and emotional renditions of classic songs have garnered him recognition and broadened his creative horizons.

4. charitable Impact: Walsh's charitable efforts have been a victory in both his personal and professional lives, showcasing his desire to make a good difference in the world. His contributions to philanthropic causes, fundraising activities, and advocacy work have helped increase awareness and support for critical concerns, resulting in substantial change and motivating others to give back.

CHAPTER EIGHT

IMPACT AND INFLUENCE

Legacy in the Entertainment Industry.

Bradley John Walsh's reputation in the entertainment business is defined by his flexibility, talent, and long-term appeal in a variety of fields. Walsh's prominent appearances in television and cinema, as well as his successful music career and humanitarian initiatives, have made an indelible impression on both fans and other celebrities.

1. Versatility as a Performer: Bradley John Walsh has excelled in a variety of roles across many mediums. Walsh's ability to attract viewers with his charm, humor, and genuineness has reinforced his image as a versatile

performer capable of commanding the screen in a variety of genres, ranging from riveting acting performances in dramas and criminal procedurals to engaging game show hosting roles.

2. Iconic TV presenter: Bradley John Walsh, presenter of "The Chase," is well-known for his entertaining approach and affinity with participants. His contagious energy, quick wit, and genuine excitement for the game have helped the show maintain its long appeal, making it one of the most-watched quiz shows on British television. Walsh's position as host of "The Chase" solidified his

reputation as an iconic television personality and popular character in British television.

3. Acclaimed Actor: Walsh has received critical praise for his appearances in television dramas and soap operas, demonstrating his variety and brilliance. His portrayals of Danny Baldwin in "Coronation Street" and Detective Sergeant Ronnie Brooks in "Law & Order: UK" demonstrated his ability to express depth and emotion, cementing his status as a respected actor in the business.

4. Successful Music Career: Bradley John Walsh's beautiful voice and passionate renditions of classic songs have led to success in the music industry, alongside his triumphs in television and movies. His albums "Chasing Dreams," "When You're Smiling," and "Anticipation" were well-received by critics and commercially successful. Walsh's music career has broadened his creative horizons and demonstrated his skill as a versatile entertainer capable of captivating audiences with his musical performances.

5. Philanthropic effect: Walsh's legacy includes philanthropic and charity undertakings, proving his dedication to make a beneficial effect on the world. Walsh's support for healthcare organizations, children's welfare projects, education programs, and animal welfare causes has motivated others to give back and donate to worthy causes, establishing a legacy of compassion, generosity, and empathy.

FANBASE AND PUBLIC PERCEPTIONS

Bradley John Walsh has a devoted fan following and a strong public image due to his numerous abilities, engaging personality, and honest manner both on and off film. His approachable charisma, honesty, and down-to-earth demeanor have won over audiences of all ages, adding to his immense popularity and enduring appeal.

1. varied Appeal: Bradley John Walsh has a varied fan base that reflects his appeal as an entertainer. Walsh's

multifaceted abilities appeal to audiences of many backgrounds and interests, from die-hard fans of his acting performances to devoted watchers of "The Chase" to supporters of his musical career. His ability to connect with viewers on various levels leads to his large following and global appeal.

2. Bradley John Walsh is known for his engaging attitude, which includes warmth, humor, and genuine passion. Walsh's captivating appearance and contagious energy attract audiences regardless of whether he is a television host, actor, or musician,

bringing them into his world and building close bonds with followers. His personable personality and genuine appeal have made him a popular figure in the entertainment business.

3. Genuine Demeanor: Walsh's genuine and down-to-earth personality has gained him respect and appreciation from fans and peers alike. Despite his success, he stays grounded, frequently expressing humility and thankfulness for the chances he has in the entertainment world. Walsh's honest personality appeals to audiences, who value his

genuineness and authenticity in a profession that is sometimes defined by artifice and pretense.

4. Fan Engagement: Bradley John Walsh connects with his fans through social media, public appearances, and fan gatherings. He takes the time to engage with fans, replying to comments, providing personal insights, and thanking them for their support. Walsh's sincere contacts with fans enhance their bond with him and develop a feeling of community among his followers.

5. Bradley John Walsh's public impression is good, with praise for his abilities, sincerity, and contributions to the entertainment business. He is widely recognized as a versatile and competent entertainer, renowned for his riveting performances, engaging hosting manner, and moving musical renditions. Walsh's reputation as a real and personable personality strengthens his public image, appealing him to viewers and winning him the respect of his industry peers.

AWARDS AND ACCOLADES

Bradley John Walsh's successful career in the entertainment business has earned him several prizes and distinctions, which recognize his brilliance, flexibility, and contributions to various aspects of the entertainment industry. Walsh's amazing collection of work, which includes acting, presenting, and singing, has been praised by colleagues, reviewers, and audiences alike, garnering him recognition and accolades on various platforms.

1. National Television Awards: Bradley. John Walsh has garnered several nominations for the National Television Awards, one of the UK's most prominent television award events. His nominations include Best Presenter for his involvement on "The Chase" and Best Drama Performance for his work in shows such as "Law & Order: UK."

British Soap Awards: Walsh's depiction of Danny Baldwin in "Coronation Street" won him accolades for Best Newcomer and Villain of the Year. His captivating performance in the long-running soap opera was lauded by both reviewers and spectators, garnering him respect within the soap opera genre.

2. Music Week Awards: Bradley John Walsh's CDs, which include "Chasing Dreams," "When You're Smiling," and "Anticipation," have been commercially successful and critically acclaimed. While Walsh's music career has not typically been recognized in major music award ceremonies, fans and reviewers have embraced it, with his albums hitting the top of the UK charts and obtaining certifications for sales successes.

3. Theatre Awards: Laurence Olivier Awards: Walsh has demonstrated his skill as a stage actor with his appearances in many shows. While he has not personally garnered Laurence Olivier prizes, his contributions to the theatre have been acknowledged, with shows in which he has participated winning nominations and prizes at prominent theatre celebrations.

4. Special Recognition: Bradley John Walsh has garnered Special Recognition honors for his services to the television business as a diverse performer and adored personality, including at TV Choice honors. These

awards recognize his influence and continuing appeal with fans across a variety of television programs and genres.

5. Honorary Awards & Degrees: Bradley John Walsh has received honorary degrees from colleges and institutes in recognition of his services to the arts and entertainment, albeit these are not standard entertainment awards. These honors recognize his accomplishments as a multidimensional entertainer and his commitment to his industry.

CONCLUSION

Bradley John Walsh's Enduring Legacy

Bradley John Walsh's career in the entertainment industry demonstrates his tremendous skill, flexibility, and lasting effect as a versatile performer. From his breakout appearances in television dramas to his career as a television host, singer, and philanthropist, Walsh has captured viewers with his charm, honesty, and true love of his work.

Walsh has overcome obstacles, celebrated successes, and left a lasting impact in the entertainment industry. His ability to connect with audiences on various levels, whether through sincere acting performances, engaging hosting, soulful musical renditions, or humanitarian activities, demonstrates his long-term popularity and impact as an artist.

As Bradley John Walsh continues to thrill and inspire audiences, his reputation as a versatile and adored personality in the entertainment business is cemented. Walsh's contributions to the arts and devotion to make a positive effect in the world will be remembered for years, whether on movie, stage, or in the hearts of his admirers.

Printed in Great Britain
by Amazon